Weekly Reader Children's Book Club presents

SNOOPY and the RED BARON

Charles M. Schulz

HOLT, RINEHART AND WINSTON
New York / Chicago / San Francisco

Here's the World War I flying ace posing beside his Sopwith "Camel."

**The Red Baron has been reported
in the vicinity of Saint-Mihiel.
I must bring him down.
"Switch off!" cries my mechanic.
"Coupez!" I reply. "Contact?"
"Contact it is!"**

"I think my dog has finally flipped!"

Here I am flying high over France in my Sopwith "Camel" searching for the infamous Red Baron!

Suddenly antiaircraft fire begins to burst below my plane. "Archie" we call it.

"Nyahh, nyahh, nyahh! You can't hit me!"

Actually, tough flying aces never said, "Nyahh, nyahh, nyahh!"

Good grief! What's that? It's the Red Baron! He's on my tail!

A stream of tracer bullets cuts across my lower right wing...

"Give my regards to Broadway!"

**As my plane strikes the ground,
I leap from the cockpit!**

Right in my supper dish....How embarassing!

"Curse you, Red Baron!"

Here's the World War I pilot asleep in his bunk being awakened to fly another dawn patrol.

"Good morning, chaps! Another important mission today, eh what? But, I dare say they all are important, eh what?"

Drat this fog! It's bad enough
having to fight the Red Baron
without having to fly in weather
like this. When I get back I'm
going to write a letter to
President Wilson!

Ah, the sun has broken through...
I can see the woods of Montsec
below...And what's that? It's a
Fokker Triplane!

"Ha! This time I've got you, Red
Baron! This time you've met
your match!"

"I hate that Red Baron!"

**The scene: An aerodrome some-
where in France. The World War I
flying ace is asleep on his bunk.
Little does he realize that he is
about to face the most terrible
experience of his life!**

"Good morning, ground crew!"

Here's the pilot standing next to
his Sopwith "Camel" chatting
with his faithful mechanics. Even
at this early hour, they admire
his calm courage.

"Switch off!" "Coupez!" "Contact?" "Contact!"

Soon I am flying high over
France. I can see the little city
of Pont-a-Mousson below...

**My strategy today is to cross
the enemy lines near Verdun...I
must find the Red Baron, and
bring him down!**

"All right, Red Baron! Where are you? You can't hide forever!"

"Aaugh! There he is! He's diving down out of the sun! He's tricked me again!"

"I've got to run! Come on, Sopwith Camel, let's go! Go, Camel, go!!!"

"I can't shake him! He's riddling my plane with bullets! It bursts into flames!"

"Curse you, Red Baron!"

"I'm coming in right over the trees!"

"AAUGH!"

Here's the World War I pilot
trapped behind enemy lines.

"I'll never make it back! I'll be
captured, and shot at dawn!
I never should have left the
Daisy Hill Puppy Farm!"

"I miss my buddies!"

That night I sneak through
abandoned trenches.

By day I sleep on haystacks.

**Dusk approaches...I must be
on my way!**

"Good grief! A sentry!"

I'll sneak up on him, grab him
by the arm, and fling him over
my back....Easy now...Mustn't
let him see me....Easy...

Okay, here he goes! One big
flip, and over he goes! This is
it...One big flip! Over he goes!
One big flip! Okay, here he goes!

Here's the World War I pilot continuing to make his way back through enemy lines.

Oh, no! More barbed wire! I'll
have to make a run for it,
and try to get through before
the machine gunners see me!

"What was that?" "I'm not sure, but I think it was a World War I pilot going through some barbed wire..."

"Ah! My journey is almost over...."

What's this? A small French farm house!

"Ah, mademoiselle...Do not be
afraid....I am a pilot with the
Allies....My plane was shot down
by the Red Baron..."

She does not understand ze English....Ah, but she will understand that I am a handsome young pilot...And she? She is a beautiful French girl...

"Soup? Ah, yes, mademoiselle...
That would be wonderful! A little
potato soup, and I will be on
my way..."

But how can I bear to leave her?
Perhaps someday I can return...
"Au revoir, mademoiselle...Au
revoir!" Ah, what a pity....Her
heart is breaking. "Do not cry, my
little one....Do not cry..."

"Farewell! Farewell!"

"Curse the Red Baron and his kind! Curse the wickedness in this world! Curse the evil that causes all this unhappiness!"

**Here's the World War I flying
ace back at the aerodrome in
France....He is exhausted
and yet he does not sleep, for one
thought runs continuously
through his mind...**

"Someday I'll get you, Red Baron!"